# TRASHFORMATIONS

# TRASHFORMATIONS

## RECYCLED MATERIALS IN CONTEMPORARY AMERICAN ART AND DESIGN

Lloyd E. Herman

Whatcom Museum of History and Art

This book was published in connection with an exhibition and national tour arranged by the Whatcom Museum of History and Art entitled *Trashformations: Recycled Materials in Contemporary American Art and Design*. The exhibition was supported by grants from the Washington State Arts Commission and the Institute of Museum Services, Washington, D.C. The publication was supported by a major grant from the Whatcom Museum Docents, with additional support provided by Doug and Dale Anderson.

Coordinated by John Olbrantz

Designed and typeset by Phil Kovacevich

Edited by Kathy Reigstad

Printed and bound in China

Front cover: Rik Nelson, *Clear Cut* (detail), 1994-95, plastic containers, 78 x 78".

Inside front/back cover: John Garrett, *Wastepaper/Wallpaper*, 1994, colored newspaper ads, Johnson Wax product packaging, 120 x 168".

Title page: Clayton Bailey, *Marilyn Monrobot*, 1989, aluminum, chrome, light, 60 x 20 x 20".

Back cover: Kiff Slemmons, *Protection #2*, 1992, pencils, silver, copper, brass, mirror, leather, horsehair, 22 x 9".

Library of Congress Catalog Card Number 97-62117
ISBN 0-9385506-04-8 softcover,  ISBN 0-295-97720-5 hardcover

Hardcover edition distributed by
University of Washington Press
P.O. Box 50096
Seattle, Washington 98145-5096

# TABLE OF CONTENTS

# PREFACE

It was in 1994 that Lloyd Herman, director emeritus of the Renwick Gallery in Washington, D.C., first proposed the idea for an exhibition on recycling in contemporary American art and design. Lloyd had been gathering material for at least a decade, but it was not until he moved to Washington state in the late 1980s and established himself as an independent curator that he approached the Whatcom Museum of History and Art with his concept for the exhibition.

There were several good reasons to pursue Lloyd's idea. First, the exhibition seemed to meet a number of the criteria that we look at in determining the feasibility and viability of a project. *Trashformations: Recycled Materials in Contemporary American Art and Design*, as we came to title the exhibition, stressed originality and innovation (two of the trademarks of Whatcom Museum of History and Art exhibitions); had the potential to make a significant contribution to scholarship in the field; featured the work of a number of important artists (many of whom had never been seen before in the region); and included objects of the highest artistic quality.

Second, we had worked with Lloyd on several occasions in the early 1990s and had enjoyed a successful and fruitful relationship with him. In 1991, he organized *From the Woods: Washington Wood Artists*, an exhibition of work by sixteen contemporary wood artists from different parts of Washington state. The following year, we asked him to curate *Clearly Art: Pilchuck's Glass Legacy*, a history of the Pilchuck Glass School in Stanwood, Washington, and an assessment of its impact on the studio glass movement in the United States. The former exhibition traveled to two venues in Washington state, and the latter enjoyed a highly successful national tour.

Finally, as an institution housed in four recycled buildings (including an 1892 city hall and a structure that was the original Ford dealership in town), and located in a city and state with a long history of environmental activism and awareness, it seemed highly appropriate that the Whatcom Museum of History and Art in Bellingham, Washington, should organize the exhibition, publication, and national tour.

On behalf of the Board of Directors and staff, we would like to express our thanks and appreciation to a number of people without whose help this project would not have been possible. We would like to thank Lloyd Herman for bringing his exhibition idea to the Whatcom Museum of History and Art for our consideration and review. We are further indebted to him for his thoughtful selection of artists and objects in the exhibition, and for his insightful and highly readable essay that graces the pages of this publication.

We would also like to express our thanks and appreciation to Phil Kovacevich for his beautiful design of the exhibition catalogue, and to Kathy Reigstad for her skillful editing of Mr. Herman's essay.

A project of this magnitude would not have been possible without the full support of the artists and lenders to the exhibition. While we cannot thank each one individually, their names appear in other parts of this book. In addition, we would like to thank the many institutions—from Oregon and New Hampshire to Texas and Alabama—that agreed to book the exhibition on its national tour.

Finally, and by no means least, we would like to thank the Washington State Arts Commission and the Institute of Museum Services for their support of the exhibition and national tour, and the Whatcom Museum Docents and Doug and Dale Anderson for their support of the exhibition catalogue. Without their commitment and financial support, *Trashformations: Recycled Materials in Contemporary American Art and Design* would not have come to fruition.

**Mary Pettus**
Director

**John Olbrantz**
Deputy Director

# INTRODUCTION

"Recycle" is a relatively new word, but virtually every citizen of this country knows it. Before we learned to "recycle," though, we reused what wasn't yet worn out. Born during the Great Depression, I learned firsthand about frugality as a child during World War II. My family carefully folded the wrapping paper from gifts to reuse on other occasions. For the war effort my sister and I saved rubber bands and foil gum wrappers; both were collected and recycled. My parents called me "Junkyard Joe" and joked that I would grow up to be a junkman. In a way I did: I worked in the "nation's attic"—the Smithsonian Institution—for twenty years, mostly as director of the Renwick Gallery, where I became sensitized to creative work from castoffs.

Today I feel that I'm part of the consumer cycle, trying to get as much use as possible out of everything before I toss it or donate it to a charity thrift store. Not only do I recycle newspapers and voluminous amounts of junk mail, I also save junk mail printed on only one side, later using the blank side to print file copies of computer-generated letters or to photocopy outgoing mail for my files. When I receive business reply envelopes without the postage indicia, I relabel and stamp them for use with bill payments. While I cook a meal, I have in mind another one planned from the leftovers. And, like many others who browse through thrift stores and consignment shops, and trawl city streets in BMWs and Cadillacs on weekends looking for yard sales, I've joined the search for the serendipitous "find" in the discards of others. It's like "antiquing" but a bit closer to the bottom of the food chain.

In the past fifty years we've seen the world's natural resources diminish and grow more precious, while as consumers we've needed larger and larger landfills to hold our discarded trash. Yet while most of us were throwing away cans, bottles, and worn-out shoes— and before recycling became public policy—artists and craftspeople were already seeing the creative possibilities in refuse. Everyone's family probably has a cherished quilt made from scrap fabrics, or a woven or braided rag rug, but in the last few decades creative people have increasingly made a deliberate choice to make art—whether functional or merely beautiful or surprising—from discards.

In the twenty years since I first became interested in this growing field, I've collected newspaper and magazine articles, gallery announcements, exhibition catalogues, and other references to artists and the objects they make from "junk." I'm grateful to the Whatcom Museum of History and Art, its director, Mary Pettus, and its deputy director, John Olbrantz, for giving me the opportunity to share my passion for creative reuse with a national audience in this traveling exhibition.

Today the number of artists, craftspeople, and product designers who see new possibilities in the stuff that others throw out is so great that the task of selecting only eighty objects for this exhibition was truly daunting. Museums and galleries that had organized more regional exhibitions than this one were generous in sharing with me the address lists of artists whose work they had shown. I'm especially grateful to Paul Schneider, owner of Twist Gallery, Portland, Oregon; Jennifer Atkinson, guest curator at the Clark Gallery, Lincoln, Massachusetts; Dorothy Globus, curator at the Fashion Institute of Technology, New York City; Lois Lambert of the Gallery of Functional Art, Santa Monica, California; Tom and Barbara Johnson, Johnson Design Studio, Seattle, Washington, founders and co-directors of the International Design Resource Awards Competition; and Judith Arango, president of the Arango Design Foundation, Miami, Florida, for their help. Their lists, coupled with addresses I had saved over the years, made it possible for me to personally invite nearly three hundred makers to let me consider their objects made from postconsumer recycled materials and found objects.

Notices in four national periodicals directed to artists and craftspeople opened the floodgates to hundreds more who wanted me to examine their creative reuse of castoffs. It took six full days to screen the slides interested artists sent me, and from those thousands of objects I selected four hundred that I really liked, then reduced that number to the eighty that made the greatest sense as an exhibition.

There have already been major exhibitions both of international product design from recycled materials and of world folk art. This exhibition begins with a reminder of some early examples of found objects in art and design and ends with a look at the hope and promise of recycling in industry. The focus of its big middle section isn't on funky assemblages; they're fairly familiar. This exhibition examines somewhat more refined objects, transformed from trash into treasures that sometimes tell stories or merely amaze us with their beauty or ingenuity. I hope that you not only will be entertained by my choices but will renew your own efforts to reduce your consumption of our world's resources and to repair, reuse, and recycle!

**Lloyd E. Herman**

**Unknown**
*Crazy Quilt*
1900
Tie and dress silks, potato sacks
68 x 66"

# TRASHFORMATIONS
## Recycled Materials in American Art and Design

**Pieced quilts and rag rugs are our American heritage.** Who hasn't seen a beautiful crazy quilt made from scraps of satin and velvet and other rich fabrics—scraps that were too lovely to throw away? Quilts are the most enduring reminder of our heritage of recycling in America, along with rugs made from strips of fabric hooked into patterns, or braided or woven in strips. The latter can still be purchased new today, but now they are usually woven of new fabric scraps discarded by textile mills.

**For decades we've taken for granted used cars and old houses.** Is there anyone alive who has always lived in new houses or driven only new cars? Our very heritage seems to be exemplified by grand old buildings that were too big or too beautiful to tear down when they outlived their original purpose; a new use had to be found for them. Today we take for granted that dignified bank buildings serve well as restaurants and stores and that schools make good retirement homes or community centers. The Archie Bray Foundation

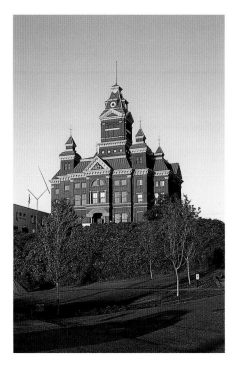

The original City Hall in Bellingham, Washington, built in 1892, currently houses the Whatcom Museum of History and Art.

for the Ceramic Arts near Helena, Montana, one of the nation's foremost ceramics schools, utilizes an old brickyard and its buildings, as do two other ceramics facilities—the Bemis Project in Omaha, Nebraska, and the Watershed Center of the Ceramic Arts in North Edgecomb, Maine. Old buildings may be remodeled to make them seem more up-to-date, but increasingly we savor old structures, cars, and other manufactured and handmade things precisely because they allow us to remember our past and remind us that our heritage is important. We're learning that the "built" environment may have been constructed better even as little as twenty years ago than it is today. Economics has always been a factor in recycling. Who once said that "an antique is something that costs more used than it did new"? Today, virtually *everything* costs more, so it makes sense to recycle materials, adapt buildings to new uses while preserving their architectural integrity, and make new products from old ones.

Marcel Duchamp
*Bicycle Wheel*
1951 (third version
after lost original
of 1913)
Metal wheel, painted
wood stool
50½ x 25½ x 16½"
Collection of the
Museum of Modern
Art, New York. The
Sidney and Harriet
Janis Collection.

**Recycling isn't limited to "folk" art.** Quilts and rag rugs may be the most familiar examples of recycling in the visual arts, but the history of art in this century is replete with examples in the "fine" arts as well as the crafts. Artists are usually the first to look at one thing and see creative possibilities in how it might resemble another. When French artist Marcel Duchamp exhibited a steel rack for drying wine bottles as a sculpture in 1914, he paved the way for future artists to use manufactured objects that could be appreciated for their visual quality in a new context. *Bottle Rack* may have been Duchamp's first "readymade"—"a common object raised to the level of a work of art through the process of appropriation"[1]—but it was preceded by simple assemblages made from more than a single "found" object. *Roue de Bicyclette,* 1913—composed of a bicycle's front wheel mounted on a wooden stool—was described by Walter Hopps as "the first major incidence of wholly non-art elements paradoxically challenging the esthetic frame of reference."[2]

Duchamp is associated with the Dada movement, "an international movement that climaxed modernism's rejection of traditional art forms and expressed the disillusionment of many artists during World War II . . . [incorporating] all the arts in its antiesthetic, anti-rational nihilism."[3] Dada was already established in Zürich and Paris when Duchamp learned of it in 1916, the year it was given a name. New York formed a Dada group, and the influence there of Duchamp lasted after his return to Europe in 1921.

Other artists incorporated found objects in collages and assemblages but were more aligned artistically with Surrealism or, in the case of Pablo Picasso and Georges Braque, Cubism. Surrealist Max Ernst's montage album, *La Femme 100 Têtes,* influenced American artist Joseph Cornell to create enigmatic, dreamlike constructions that often took meaning from such elements as music scores, celestial images, and spheres, maps, birds, and broken goblets—"boxed poetry," some have called them. Author Dore Ashton, a longtime friend of Cornell's, recalled that the artist adopted Ernst's montage technique in 1932 and "familiarized himself with the philosophical leitmotifs of the [Surrealist] movement."[4] Cornell, who had no formal art training, called himself a designer. He thought of his works

"One day, in a rubbish heap, I found an old bicycle seat lying beside a rusted handlebar, and my mind instantly linked them together. I assembled these two objects, which everyone [then] recognized as a bull's head. The metamorphosis was accomplished, and I wish another metamorphosis would occur in the reverse sense. If my bull's head were thrown in a junk heap, perhaps one day some boy would say, 'Here's something that would make a good handlebar for my bicycle!'" —Pablo Picasso

not as constructions or sculptures or collages in the modern tradition, but as "poetic enactments, verbal bibelots, bits of static theater—anything but works of visual art."[5]

Louise Nevelson, another mid-century master of found-object art, attended in 1936 the exhibitions *Fantastic Art: Dada and Surrealism* and *Cubist and Abstract Art,* organized by

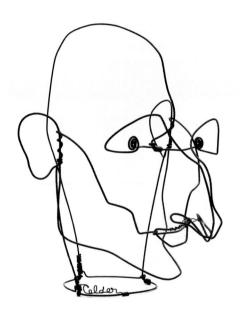

**Alexander Calder**
*Head of Michael Tapie*
ca. 1930
Wire
12 1/2"
Collection of the Elvehjem Museum of Art, University of Wisconsin, Madison

Alfred Barr at New York's Museum of Modern Art, "but it was not until 1942 that she began to construct her own unfamiliar landscapes."[6] That year her third solo exhibition "was influenced by Surrealism but not the psychoanalytic Surrealism of Breton, Magritte and Dali. She was intrigued by the surreal tableaus of isolation that could be found in window displays. . . . Nevelson's early assemblages lacked finesse of craft. They did not merely break with the tradition of familiar image reference, they also broke with the tradition of craft and materials."[7]

About the same time, other artists began to discover the creative potential of found objects. Around 1940, weaver Anni Albers and her colleague at Black Mountain College in North Carolina, Alexander Reed, made experimental jewelry from hardware and stationery store supplies. In 1946 their work was exhibited at the Museum of Modern Art in New York, and in 1949 it was shown at both the Katharine Kuh Gallery in Chicago and the Willard Gallery in New York.

The success of American artists such as Cornell, Nevelson, Albers, and Alexander Calder clearly paved the way for Robert Rauschenberg's "combine paintings" of the 1950s, which incorporated such disparate objects as a pieced quilt smeared with paint and a stuffed goat wearing a tire. Sculptors such as Mark di Suvero, in his use of welded iron and steel

"The first stimulus to make jewelry from hardware came to us from the treasure of Monte Alban, the most precious jewels from ancient Mexico. . . . We began to look around us and, still in Mexico, we found beads made of onyx, which nobody ever seemed to buy . . . we combined onyx with silver . . . and later, back in the States, we looked for new materials to use. In the 5 & 10 cents stores we discovered the beauty of washers and bobbypins. Enchanted, we stood before kitchen-sink stoppers and glass insulators, picture books and erasers. The art of Monte Alban had given us the freedom to see things detached from their use, as pure materials, worth being turned into precious objects. . . . Our greatest surprise was that others, like ourselves, did not care about the value or lack of value of our materials used, but enjoyed instead of the material value that of surprise and inventiveness, a spiritual value." —Anni Albers

**Anni Albers /
Alexander Reed**
*Necklace*
1996 (replica after
original of ca. 1945)
Sink drain, paper
clips, chain
13½ x 1 x 3"

elements found in junkyards; John Chamberlain, in his Abstract Expressionist sculpture from crushed automobiles; and painter Julian Schnabel, who collaged broken dishes to his paintings, all form the lineage of found objects recycled into art, as do many of the artists in this exhibition who combine fine-art concepts with a high level of craftsmanship.

"Nevelson gleans the forms from the detritus of society that satisfy the selectivity of her eye and from which, in a system of interdependency, she creates new images. In some respects, she is a folk artist, akin to Simon Rodia. . . ." —Arnold Glimcher

**Outside the mainstream of art, dreams are realized from junk.** Creative individuals with no academic training in art have used found objects to create complex and imaginative environments as well as independent works of art. Perhaps the most famous of these is Watts Towers, nine major sculptures built in Los Angeles by Simon Rodia, an Italian immigrant who purchased a triangular lot in 1921 and began to construct his masterpiece. He worked alone for thirty-three years covering a structural steel framework with mortar studded with a mosaic of broken tiles. His colorful constructions recall the undulating, tile-encrusted walls of Antonio Gaudí's Parc Güell in Barcelona—the heritage that also informs Isaiah Zagar's art in this exhibition.

All over the United States others like Rodia, working obsessively with the variety of used materials available to them, have created works of art. At least five in California, New Mexico, and Kansas are monuments listed in the National Register of Historic Places; nine

Isaiah Zagar
*A Day in America*
1996
Plywood, sheet rock,
mosaic
96¾ x 96¾ x 6"

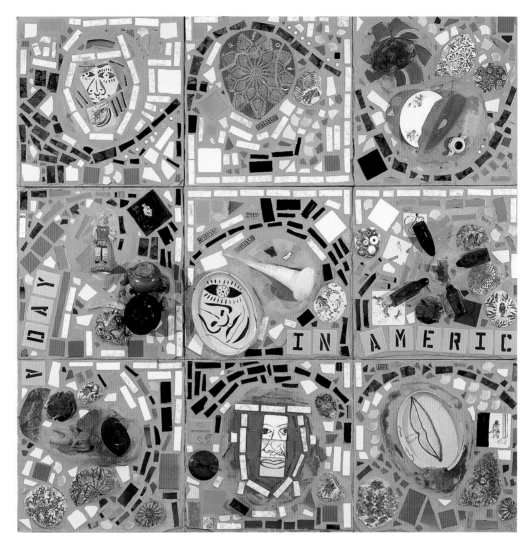

in California are state landmarks. "Litto, the Pope Valley [California] Hubcap King" has worked since 1957 to create a hubcap "ranch" from more than three thousand hubcaps. Signpost Forest, found along a remote Yukon section of the Alaska Highway, was begun in 1942 with an ordinary directional sign at Watson Lake. As visitors have added mementos of their hometowns, the Forest has grown to five acres and an estimated twelve thousand signs. Along another thoroughfare—Highway 28 near Ephrata, Washington—Pioneer Muffler hosts a family of life-sized freestanding sculptures—father, mother, child, and a Pink Panther—all constructed of welded and painted mufflers, exhaust pipes, and other miscellaneous car parts. Tooling along those highways, you're also likely to see somewhere an old car encrusted with plastic toys, beads, or other detritus; it would be one of hundreds of such automobiles decorated by artists in what has become known as the Art Car movement.

Washington, like many states, boasts a variety of such road-side attractions: Emil Gehrke's garden of windvanes and found objects at Grand Coulee; Dick Elliott and Jane Orleman's Dick and Jane's Spot in Ellensburg, with yard art made from a variety of discards; and Dick Tracy's Centralia yard with its ghostly white sculptures, many made from the formed Styrofoam used to pack small appliances. Even in urban Seattle, the Walker Rock Garden in West Seattle, the Garden of Everyday Miracles in Fremont, and the Jello Mold Building—its façade ornamented with aluminum kitchen molds until it was demolished in 1997—are delightful surprises.

Tressa "Grandma" Prisbrey built twenty-two structures from bottles acquired from daily trips to the local landfill near Simi Valley, California. When she began construction several decades ago, Bottle Village was made to house her collections of pencils, seashells, and dolls. Efforts to preserve her creation, and other outsider-art environments like it, require large sums of money (and generally involve zoning and other legal wrangles).

**Don Baum**
*The Rider*
1989
Paint by number on canvas, wood
16 x 15¼ x 7½"

**Mildred Howard**
*Memory Garden I*
1991
Wood, paint, glass bottles
26½ x 27¼ x 31¼"

Bottles have captivated more than one artist: in Canada's British Columbia, two bottle "castles" have been constructed. In Duncan, George Plumb built George's Glass Castle and Medieval Mini Golf in 1961 from 200,000 beer and liquor bottles. Another castle, built by retired funeral director David Henderson Brown in Boswell, is made from 500,000 square embalming fluid bottles.

**Recycled materials save trees in new construction.** Bottles seemed like such a good structural idea that in 1960 Alfred Heineken, head of the Dutch brewery that bears his name, developed the WOBO (for "WOrld BOttle"). The Dutch island of Curaçao in the West Indies had both a glut of empty beer bottles and a housing shortage. Heineken enlisted a young architect, John Habraken, to design a bottle that could be used as a brick, self-aligning and interlocking to eliminate the need for mortar. Unfortunately, the heavier bottle was more costly to manufacture, didn't appeal to beer drinkers, and had to be laid on its side (the weakest orientation), requiring a special silicon-cement mortar. The idea was scrapped.[8]

Housing from recycled materials has captivated others through the years. In Pigeon Cove, Massachusetts, Elis F. Stenman, with the help of his family, in 1922 began to prepare Boston newspapers for the construction of an unusual house. When the twenty-year project was finished, the walls consisted of two hundred and fifteen thicknesses of newspaper. The house, now open to tourists, is furnished with a clock, piano, desk, table, and chairs all made from rolled-up newspaper.[9]

**Wharton Esherick**
*Hammer-handle Chair*
1938
Hickory, canvas belting
32½ x 20½ x 21"

Perhaps this application isn't so surprising, given newspaper's long history of use in housing—shredded and blown into walls as insulation, reprocessed into wallboard, and so on. In fact, reprocessed materials such as newspaper are finding new possibilities in contemporary housing construction. Montana architect Steven Loken's house on the outskirts of Missoula boasts not only insulation derived from newspaper, but ceramic floor tiles made from used fluorescent bulbs and other tiles made from used windshield glass. Much of the wood used in construction was either salvaged stock or "composite" lumber (made from the chips of the slender trees that are usually discarded). From the foundation to the roof, the conventional-looking split-level house is made almost entirely of recycled materials. Since the average wood-framed house uses as much as eleven thousand board feet of lumber—enough, stacked end to end, to top the Empire State Building and both World Trade Center towers combined—reliance on recycled materials is environmentally sound.[10]

Less conventional are the houses designed by New Mexico architect Michael Reynolds, who uses disposable beverage cans as bricks at Rolor, a community of low-cost experimental homes near Taos. His own home, like the one he designed for actor Dennis Weaver, was built largely of cans and mud-packed tires.[11]

Use of recycled materials isn't new, nor is it exclusive to the United States. During the Great Depression the U.S. government created jobs in public works and other sectors, including the Works Projects Administration. WPA projects provided employment for— among many others—writers, painters, and sculptors. In the crafts, WPA sponsored a toy-making project in Connecticut, fabric-printing and furniture construction in Ohio, and the employment of Seneca Indians in New York State to recreate objects from the Iroquois culture. One of the most spectacular WPA projects was the design and construction of Timberline Lodge, a ski resort on Mount Hood in Oregon. Virtually everything in the lodge was handmade, from the furniture, rugs, bedspreads, and draperies in the guest rooms to mosaics and forged-iron gates and door hardware throughout the building.

Recycling played a strong role in the design and construction of the lodge, as well as in its embellishments. Telephone poles were used as supports in the building and carved into animal-topped newel posts to decorate stairways. Railway iron was forged into log grates and decorative hardware. Sixty years after its opening by President Franklin D. Roosevelt in 1936, it remains one of the nation's most remarkable projects in which art was wedded to architecture in a strongly vernacular building.

In timber-scarce Japan, brand-new buildings are being constructed of secondhand wood—among them, Atsuo Hoskino's House of Used Lumber, on the outskirts of Tokyo. Closer to home, the vast new house recently constructed for Microsoft founder Bill Gates required no trees to be cut; the architect recycled about one-half-million board feet from sheds built in the 1920s for a now closed lumber company in Longview, Washington.[12]

**Recycling becomes public policy.** Americans relished prosperity after the Great Depression and World War II ended. As new goods flooded the markets in the 1950s, that sense of prosperity spawned the freedom to be wasteful. For the first time, many families had disposable income to spend on leisure activities and could "keep up with the Joneses" by owning the newest gadgets and machines (and throwing out the old). Production of new goods was no problem, but consumption of goods at the rate new goods were produced was. Obsolescence became a byword for manufacturers; styles changed quickly, so that last year's model—which had seemed so fashionable prior to purchase—was soon out of date. Excessive and unnecessary packaging, disposables such as diapers and plastic cups, and a plethora of new plastics that wouldn't disintegrate in dumps or landfills added to the problem. In only one generation, America was transformed from a nation of savers to a nation of wasters. Designer Victor Papanek named it the "Kleenex Culture."[13]

During the counterculture movement of the 1960s, numerous younger Americans sought the simplicity of rural life, shunning corporate greed, intrusive government, and the wasteful ways of modern life. Concern for preserving the natural environment went hand in hand with a desire to reduce the wastefulness of ever-new consumer product lines. The

**Sam Verts**
*Can Console*
1980
Cans, labels, metal
armature
34½ x 49 x 25"

first Earth Day, in 1970, was precipitated by publication eight years earlier of Rachel Carson's *Silent Spring*—a wake-up call to Americans about environmental destruction. In *Refuse: Good Everyday Design from Reused and Recycled Materials*, authors Suzette Sherman and Peter Stathus noted the impact of that event:

"Within six months [of the first Earth Day], 3,000 community recycling centers were active across America. Unfortunately, during the following decade spending on these programs was almost entirely eliminated until public action peaked again in 1988 amid reports from the Office of Technology Assessment which warned of declining landfill capacity, overuse of virgin materials, and the presence of toxic substances in discarded products.' . . . The next year the [Environmental Protection Agency] issued its first guidelines for recycled materials and there was a rush to adopt collection programs."[14]

Newspapers were the first to be recycled, after consumers learned that the Sunday *New York Times* required the pulping of seventy-five thousand trees. Glass bottles and aluminum cans were the next items to be collected in the community recycling centers that sprang up in parking lots of suburban grocery stores. And, while in many states refillable beer and pop bottles had been worth a penny or two to schoolkids who returned them to stores, "bottle bills" enacted in several states required a deposit on all bottles to keep them out of landfills. Unfortunately, the supply of recycled papers, bottles, and cans outpaced the demand for them. It was only when government at all levels awakened to the problems of both trash incineration and the diminishing sites for landfills for disposal of garbage that official support of recycling grew—and with that support came the purchase of recycled goods, helping the market for such goods to catch up to the supply.

Now recycling is well on its way to becoming a success story. "Most instrumental in this success have been governmental procurement programs for recycled paper. About seventy-three percent of the U.S. population now lives in states with recycled-content laws for newsprint." Government is involved in other ways as well. In fact, "most collection programs are part of municipal waste management and are subsidized by local government. Subsidies have been necessary because in the past materials typically sold for less than the cost to collect, transport and prepare them for market."[15]

This is not to say that uses have been found for all recycled materials, or that the demand for new products made from salvaged materials has caught up with the supply. "The recent increased consumption of scrap aluminum, paper, and plastics (up seventy percent from the year before) has had little to do with consumer demand. It is caused largely by an increase in exports. . . . Only in the last year have a growing economy and increased demand for export to Europe and Asia sent prices to record heights. Prices are likely to fall just as quickly unless the market for recoverables can be stabilized.[16]

The market also needs to venture into uncharted territory. "Today technology permits recycling of only five of the forty-five or so plastics currently available on the market. Bear in mind that of these five, only two percent are finally reborn as new products. . . . A huge future market for this glut of unused compounds awaits research and development by scientists and entrepreneurs of vision."[17]

(opposite)
**Roland Simmons**
*Lumalight Lamps*
1997
Acid-free wastepaper
Dimensions vary

**Colin Reedy**
*Loop Seat*
1993
Recycled plastic, stainless steel, rubber nautical bumper
27½ x 22 x 31"

Increasingly, as the small group of objects manufactured from recycled materials in this exhibition demonstrates, attractive and functional new goods should be able to compete successfully in the marketplace. No one need compromise aesthetic or performance standards in the products they buy to enlarge the great cycle of creative reuse. However, to really make a difference in the growing global mountain of trash, we must work toward major shifts in attitudes and values in individuals as well as industries.

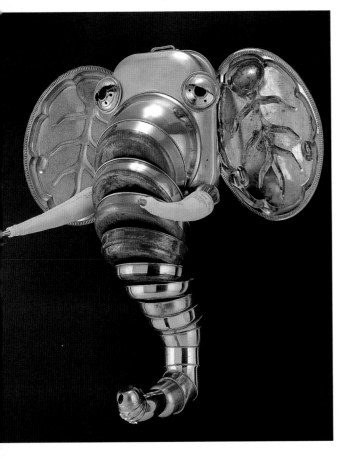

**Artists and designers often lead the way.** This exhibition, mostly of unique works of art, doesn't mean to suggest that artists can make a significant dent in our national trash mountains by recycling interesting objects or materials. In their innovative application of materials, though, creative people—artists, designers, craftspeople—often find solutions that lead to products that can and do use quantities of trash from landfills. In Third World countries, shortages of virgin materials often force craftspeople to use society's castoffs. Who hasn't seen small suitcases from Haiti that are clad with printed tin from cans, or enjoyed a cool drink from heavy Mexican blown glassware colored distinctively by the bottles melted to make it? Mexican craftspeople still cut up old tires to make soles for their huaraches and roll strips of colorful photographs cut from magazines into beads for tourist necklaces. All over the world, rubber tires are used for children's swings, cut into planters for flowers, or made into carriers for coal or wood.

**Jim Opasik**
*Pan-A-Phant*
1993
Recycled kitchen utensils, pans, pastry bags
36 x 33 x 22"

**Al Honig**
*Primitive #5*
1995
Mixed media
15 x 13 x 6"

**Material, meaning, and memory—these are artists' reasons for using found objects.** Many of the artists who prefer to recycle found objects in making new work like either the surface appearance of the material or its shape, or they appropriate something of the object's original meaning to tell stories in the objects they make from it. Two artists mentioned earlier, Louise Nevelson and Joseph Cornell, typify these contrasting viewpoints.

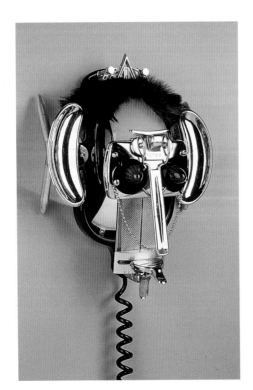

Nevelson, constructing from found wood her dreamlike abstract landscapes, selected elements only for their shapes. Emily Genauer, writing about Nevelson's 1944 exhibition of abstract wood sculptures, noted that only "in a few instances has Miss Nevelson carved her own shapes. Instead she has taken existing objects, a wooden duck decoy, a hatter's block, a chair rail, a ten pin, sanded them down and assembled them into complex constructions of astonishing interest and variety. . . ."[18] Arnold Glimcher, writing about

Leonard Streckfus
*Rhino*
1986
Can, fire hose, golf
balls, kettle, mail-
box, tire, tricycle
parts, wicker horn
30 x 21 x 30"

"My intention is to create a living image, a spirit that a-spir-ates, as opposed to a tro-phy-room carcass. I use trash as a medium where other artists might use clay or paint. One distinction might be that I find or recog-nize shapes, where an abstract artist might create a shape, or a representational artist might reproduce a shape. I approach the found shape metaphorically, asking myself, 'What does this object look like? What does it feel like? Does it, on its own, evoke some-thing else? Could it, together with other found shapes, create something new?' When put together, these objects may have no other relationship than shape and thus seem somewhat ridiculous or, to a Surrealist at heart, may appear 'beautiful, like the chance meeting of a sewing machine and an um-brella on a dissecting table,' in Lautreamont's famous phrase." —Leonard Streckfus

Nevelson in his book on the artist, added that she "views the elements or images that are combined in her work as virginal; she erases all their previous history. The elements are painted black before she begins to work with them, equipping her with an inventory of ready forms to combine them instinctively first into units and then complete walls. . . . For Nevelson, the object's original history does not exist."[19]

The reverse of Nevelson's attitude would seem to be true in the "boxed poetry" of Joseph Cornell. Except perhaps for the very boxes that contain his enigmatic tableaus, every ele-ment seems to suggest meaning, depending somewhat on what each viewer brings to it. Dore Ashton has described Cornell as "the issue of nineteenth century Romanticism. . . . [E]ach fragment, whether a china squirrel, a ship's model, wood, beads, or trifles from the sea, was significant to him. The poetic enactments which are his boxes and collages are the visible issue of this palace of dreams and associations."[20]

That poetic spirit persists in contemporary found-object art. In this exhibition, perhaps the work closest to Cornell's visual enigmas is Jeff Smith's glass-front box, hung on the wall with a hammer at its side (presumably to break the glass in case of emergency, in the manner of fire call boxes). However, what's inside the box, clearly visible, is just another hammer. Is the result humorous only, or suggestive also of futility? This piece—

**Jeff Smith**
*Hammer in Glass*
*"Emergency" Box*
1996
Wood, glass, metal
24 x 8 x 12"

in which the selection and placement of objects is carried out without physically trans-
forming them—reflects something of the Surreal.

Johanna Nitzke Marquis really does use a box in her *Hey Now What's That Sound
Everybody Look What's Going Down,* but its meaning is much more clearly understood than
in Cornell's boxed constructions. Her box is that of the *en-plein-air* painter who sets up an

Johanna Nitzke
Marquis
*Hey Now What's
That Sound
Everybody Look
What's Going Down*
1995
Watercolor, mixed
media
19 x 12¹/₄ x 2¹/₂"

easel outdoors to paint the landscape.
This landscape, painted inside the paint-
box lid, extends the image of an antique
picture postcard depicting a rustic log
bridge at its center. The artist has added
other found objects to complete her
visual plea to protect our national parks
and the natural habitat of wild animals.

Like Smith's assemblage, Joy Taylor's
*The Girl I Sawed With You Last Night*
also first evokes in viewers a smile
before we ponder its deeper meaning.
Stretching a woman's elbow-length formal glove over the blade of a handsaw
seems to be an exploration of the "what
if?" creativity evidenced by many artists'
use of found objects, and instantly
recalls Duchamp's assemblages.

Joy Taylor
*The Girl I Sawed
With You Last Night*
1992
Handsaw, glove
26 x 5 x 2"

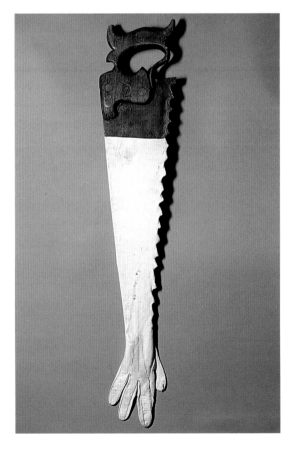

"I discovered quite by accident that
putting objects together meant putting
their meanings together as well. This is
not just a formal association based on
two objects looking alike, or their being
used for similar purposes, but the
creation of a new entity from two old
familiar presence,"[21] Taylor recounts.
The shape of the saw suggests a fore-
arm, and the contrast of a feminine
garment with a masculine tool is a wedding of opposites. The sharp sawteeth

"I began collecting discarded materials and looking
for objects with a history early on in my life as an
artist, gathering scraps off the sidewalks in New
York to glue together, first as collages, then as box
constructions, and finally as freestanding sculptures.
Trash was free, and it was beautiful, with intricate
textures and colors." —Joy Taylor

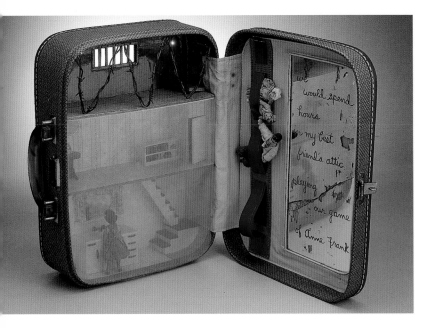

pushing through the soft glove leather suggest that this "wedding" wasn't made in heaven. "The sawing motions of the tool cut into the gentility of high society. Male sweat meets female perfume."[22]

Taylor adds, "The title comes from an old vaudeville joke, in which two magicians meet on the street. The first magician says, 'Say, who was that little short girl I sawed with you last night?' The second magician says, 'That was no little short girl, that was my half sister!'"[23]

The tableau, Cornell's favored format, is also the choice of two California artists, Gaza Bowen and Helen Cohen. Bowen's *Het Achterhuis* incorporates an old suitcase, a dollhouse figure and furniture, and barbed wire to recall how the artist and a friend, as children, imagined themselves as Anne Frank and her family hiding from the Nazis in an Amsterdam attic. Bowen sees the piece as part of an ongoing series reflecting childhood memories, built in found containers/cases. "I see them as miniature site-specific installations—where I am responding to a psychological quality that the case resonates, as well as the physical space. . . . In using recycled materials I feel I am responding to some quality that the material has absorbed during its life (previous to my finding it). This quality can be physical or psychological or often both."[24]

**Gaza Bowen**
*Het Achterhuis*
1995
Suitcase, dollhouse figure/furniture, barbed wire, lighting, scrim cloth, mirror
14½ x 16 x 12"

Helen Cohen's tableaus of domestic life are "framed" within hollowed appliances pertinent to the stories they suggest. Vacuum cleaners, plastic table radios, and kitchen appliances (such as the toaster exhibited here) look very ordinary until the viewer examines the source of light emitting from the appliance's aperture. Inside this toaster, for example, is the tiny kitchen from which it might have come, complete in detail.

**Helen Cohen**
*Sunbeam Toaster*
1996
1950s toaster,
ceramic cup and
saucer, found
objects
8 x 11 x 7"

**Helen Cohen**
*Sunbeam Toaster*
(interior view)

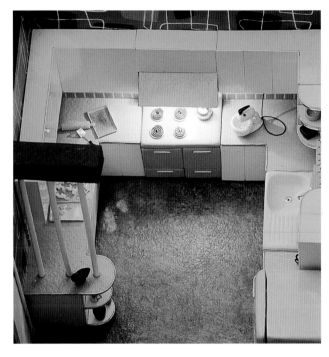

About Helen Cohen's *Miniverse,* Tina Dunkley, gallery director at Georgia State University Gallery of Art, wrote in October 1991:

"In one of Rod Serling's episodes of *The Twilight Zone* (ca. 50s/60s), you may recall a distraught couple who find themselves lost in what appears to be a deserted sub-urban town. They run frantically from house to house knocking on doors and pulling off door-knobs. Upon entering some of the homes, they discover all the furniture and cabinetry are only veneered, easily destroyed with a stroke of the hand. Towards the end, the camera scans upward leaving the exas-perated man and woman to focus on a 'little' giant girl play-ing with them on her scale model toy community. She resists the calls of her mother who soon enters the room tow-ering even farther above the reality of illusion.

Cohen's works eerily simulate a twilight zone in our conscious-ness, a consciousness full of introspection and memories. One is struck by a feeling of transition in one's physical size. When approaching any of Cohen's commonplace objects, one feels proportionate-ly correct. But, upon peering into the meticulously constructed dioramas, you are immensely enlarged, then quickly minimized to the HO size of hobby train fig-ures. At this intimate proportion you surrender yourself to nostalgia."[25]

David Gilhooly works on a similar scale, revealing the wacky sense of humor that cata-pulted him into the history of art in the 1960s with his retelling of world history and myth through tableaus of ceramic frog heroes. No longer creating in clay, he writes that "I like to use only plastic things—things from Goodwill stores especially, since they seem to have the best toys, decorator items, hobbyist paintings, and plastic frames. . . . I especially like bendies and action figures, as long as they've really been toys and not 'collectibles'

**David Gilhooly**
*Extra Guests at the
Last Supper*
1996
Plastics
10 x 20½ x 4½"

**David Gilhooly**
*Floor Show at the
Last Supper*
1996
Plastics
8⅞ x 17½ x 3½"

(toys you don't play with). I sometimes use valuable things, too, just to annoy collectors, and can imagine in some future that the toys may be worth more than my work. I also love the hideousness of plastic wall decorations—mostly from the sixties—the plastic equivalent of resin grapes and English brass plates. . . . I won't use anything else for frames. They fit. . . . The pieces are shadow boxes aligned to the Victorian ideal. I parody not art but hobby crafts."[26]

Gilhooly's *Extra Guests at the Last Supper* and *Floor Show at the Last Supper* are parodies on several levels. The cheap, mass-produced three-dimensional adaptations of Leonardo da Vinci's famous painting began as lowbrow kitsch. Gilhooly poked further fun at the cheapening of famous artwork by augmenting the adaptations with plastic toys. The result is art about kitsch about art.

Though Daniel Mack's furniture is neither diorama nor tableau, his choice and use of found objects purposefully evokes memory. "My current work also ranges into history—

**Daniel Mack**
*Rugbeater-back*
*Armchair*
1995
Maple saplings,
wicker rugbeaters
48 x 26 x 24"

the history of furniture, the history of mundane objects, and the history of chairmaking.
I've come to call these Memory Chairs. They use common objects with strong natural
forms to tell stories and evoke memories. These chairs evoke memories exactly because I
use objects, both natural and made, that most people already have some experience
with: fishing rods, hammers, boat oars. . . . I'm working with an already stored bank of
memories and associations."[27]

On a small scale, found-object jewelry often tells stories through its maker's choice of
materials. J. Fred Woell, among the foremost of found-object jewelers across the nation,

J. Fred Woell
*Pat and Fred Pin*
1992
Plastic, glass, wood,
brass, paper
1⅞ x 3 x ½"

has since the 1960s incorporated bottle caps, comic strip and photographic images, bits of broken china, and other finds into his narrative art-to-wear. It has often been personal—for example, mocking the dreams of newlyweds after divorce from his first wife and now celebrating the union with his second wife, Pat. *Pat and Fred* incorporates a plastic eyeglass lens, driftwood, a broken mirror, a door-lock part, a watch gear, and a number tack used to identify storm windows.

"This pin was created as a Christmas gift for my wife. The number twelve represents the day of our marriage, October 12, 1992. The wire elements visualize the idea of connecting each of us in that ceremony—thus the use of the names 'Pat' and 'Fred' stamped on a couple of the metal parts that make up the design. . . . The plastic eyeglass lens in this piece was one from my own prescription glasses."[28]

"Found-object 'trash' somehow ends up in my life more by serendipity than by my searching seriously for it. . . . I think that I am more obsessed with the need to recycle things that our society throws away than I am with looking for interesting 'trash.' I was an Eagle Scout and learned in those formative years as a Boy Scout that the SIGN OF A GOOD SCOUT IS NO SIGN AT ALL. I hate the fact that we waste and litter. The amount of materials that we use to package products—materials that we consider throwaway—boggles my mind."
—J. Fred Woell

Ken Bova's brooch, *Daddy's Pride and Joy,* is also a personal reminiscence made concrete. "It's both a small memorial and [a partial] portrait of my dad. . . . The photograph is one of my father bathing me in a washbasin in our backyard in Texas. . . . The 'stag' in the collage is from a Nepalese rupee that an acquaintance brought back from an expedition to Mount Everest. (My father was a devout deer hunter.) The flower is a pressed forget-me-not from a mountain trail near my home in Bozeman. The horn tip comes from one of the antlers in my dad's collection, and the 'blue moon' is a part cannibalized from a piece I did as a student. (It refers to the cliché 'once in a blue moon,' which was about how often my dad would offer praise to any of his four sons for their accomplishments, though he would brag about us to his friends.) The blue is also the color of his uniforms—he was a mail carrier and a law enforcement officer. The piece is constructed from some leftover watercolor paper, and the gold is partly recycled wedding bands."[29]

(clockwise from top)
**Ken Bova**
*Daddy's Pride and Joy*
1991
14k and 23k gold,
sterling silver,
pastel, paper, horn,
pearls, quartz,
photo, shell
3½ x 2¾"

**Lisa Fidler**
*Spinning Ouija Brooch*
1996
Mirror shards,
thesaurus pages,
sterling silver, glass,
dice, taillight plastic
3½ x ⅓"

**Rita Rubin**
*Necklace*
1996
Ancient glass shards,
yellow, red, and
white gold wire
10 x 10"

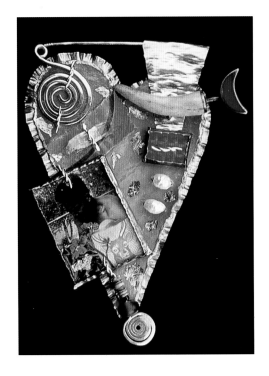

"What's exciting for me is the process of collecting bits and pieces of everyday objects—snippets of glass; plastic; photos; pages from dictionaries; pieces of metal—and from this vocabulary of snippets figuring out how to make pieces of wearable, hand-held art. I am fascinated by what objects, images, and words imply within a culture as well as cross-culturally. What do people—from artists to shopkeepers—use from the daily environment to convey a message, to express what they believe, who they are, what they sell?" —Lisa Fidler

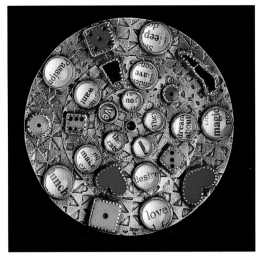

"Some years ago during a visit to Israel, I was browsing in an antique shop and found a dusty box of broken glass. Wondering why anyone would save what at first glance looked like worthless junk, I started picking through the shards. Three hours later I had set aside a bunch of pieces that I just had to have, not yet knowing what I would do with them.

I asked the shop owner what they were and he told me that they were unearthed in the many archeological digs which are ongoing in Israel and much of the Middle East. These shards were originally beautifully blown goblets, vases, dishes, etc., which took on an even more beautiful patina from having been buried for up to several thousand years. Many of the pieces are exquisitely colored and look like opal, jade, and other lovely minerals. After returning to Los Angeles I began using the shards in my jewelry and have since replenished my original purchase several times." —Rita Rubin

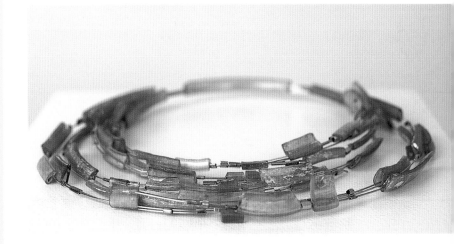

(clockwise from
top right)
**Tina Fung Holder**
*Martha Necklace*
1995
Safety pins, snap
fasteners, glass beads
¼ x 9 x 8½"

**Eric Margry**
*Blowup Bracelet with
Pump*
1996
Bicycle tire tube,
sterling silver
Bracelet: 4 x 3½ x 1"
Pump: 1⅛ x 8¼ x 1½"

**ROY**
*Mediterranean
Bracelet*
1994
Diamonds, bus stop
signs
1½ x 6⅝ x ³⁄₁₆"

**Kathy Buszkiewicz**
*Savior*
1996
U.S. currency, wood
1¾ x 6"

"The primary recycled material I use is shredded U.S. currency. Several years ago I received permission from the
federal government to use it within my work. . . . The strips
[of shredded money] are adhered to a substrate structure,
usually lathe-turned wood, in an ordered fashion to create a
pattern, a texture, or an emphasis of the work's concept . . .
[for example,] the idea of 'Value.' Being a member of our
American society, I am intrigued with cultural perceptions
regarding the worth of objects." —Kathy Buszkiewicz

"Because I was born in Holland, bicycles were my
mode of transportation. I rode my bicycle every-
where—from the tip of Norway to the Adriatic Sea. I
have fixed a lot of flat tires, and I have always found
it interesting how the patches don't stretch while the
rubber blows up around them. So I got the idea to
constrict the tire even more by wrapping wire or plac-
ing rings along the tube. I like the fact that air makes
up the largest portion of this piece and that you can
change it by how much you pump it up. Don't be
afraid to wear rubber!" —Eric Margry

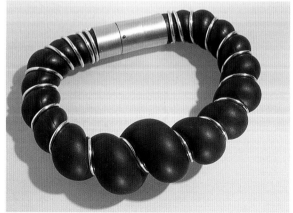

When materials that have specific, personal meaning to artists are combined with other, more neutral materials, they often take on additional narrative qualities, as the above examples show. However, most of us in the United States today share not only a collective memory but also a familiarity with cultural symbols and the symbolic qualities of commercial trademarks and logos. The persistence of advertising, and the products that become commonplace through advertising, has therefore also become part of the artist's palette. Just as Andy Warhol recognized the iconic qualities of Brillo and Campbell's Soup graphics in his art, Harriete Estel Berman found her product icon in Slim-Fast, the liquid diet in a can. Advertisers don't sell steak, they sell the sizzle, it has been said. In the case of Slim-Fast, the "sizzle" sold to dieters is a vision of how slim and attractive they will look after using the product.

**Harriete Estel Berman**
*Hourglass Figure:
The Scale of Torture*
1994
Slim-fast can and
cookie tin steel,
acrylic
3 x 12½ x 13"

In *Hourglass Figure: The Scale of Torture* (from her series "A Pedestal for a Woman to Stand On"), Berman didn't rely only on the easy recognition of Slim-Fast's distinctive red and white graphics. She added layers of meaning to the promise of slimness and beauty by fashioning a bathroom scale from the printed metal of Slim-Fast

**Harriete Estel Berman**
*Hourglass Figure:
The Scale of Torture*
(detail)

"There is a trace of Marcel Duchamp's irony in the way Berman uses language, humor and images. However, she strips away the esoteric verbal games and tension between images and words we associate with Duchamp. . . . Berman fabricates all of her objects. She doesn't enter the world of Duchamp's readymades, where a functional, mass-produced object was ultimately turned into a precious art commodity."
—C. E. Licka

cans, playing with the idea that the measure of product acceptance, in this case, is found in the user's weight loss. She cut the metal with pinking shears and then juxtaposed the Slim-Fast logo with cookie images from cookie tins in a traditional pieced-quilt format ("women's work"), raising the pinked edges to cause a user pain when she stands on the scale. In place of numbers showing the user's weight, on the scale's face are food names used to describe women—"cupcake," "honeybun," "tomato," and so on—a reminder of the deprivation of favorite foods in the cause of "beauty." But wait: the irony doesn't end there. The inside of the scale is a miniature dollhouse, yet another allusion to feminist iconography. "The inside is the part that very few people see; it is a reflection of my domestic sphere trimmed with autobiographical content."[30]

Several other artists tackle the subject of traditional "women's" roles—especially in marriage—by their choice and use of found materials. Katharine Cobey's *Loose Ends*, a wedding gown knitted from white plastic Glad kitchen bags, and Donna Rhae Marder's "quilt" made from used coffee filters both tie women to kitchen chores and refer to domestic sewing, too. Flora Walters hints at the shackles of marriage in her *Selective Service*, an apron made from wedding rings as chainmail. (Only one of the rings is real; the rest are reproductions.) Yet another wedding ensemble, *Tying the Knot* by Gloria Crouse—a garment fashioned out of plastic six-pack rings tied with selvage edges of ripstop nylon—makes more of a pun with the title than with the use of materials.

Katharine Cobey
*Loose Ends Dress
and Wreath*
1996
Cut and knitted white
Glad bags
Dress: 50 x 46 x 6"
Wreath: 12 x 12"

"I knit with garbage bags
    because they 'handle' well, knit crisply, drape fluidly,
    because they reflect light variously in different stitches,
    because they rustle + flair + cling,
    because I like irony and paradox,
    because I like to knit the silk purse from the sow's ear,
    because I can be intimate or political or incorrect with them,
    because garbage bags are not garbage,
    because I hate waste,
    because they can be transformed, and still insist on their antecedents.
For me these leaps and focuses and contradictions are exhilarating."

          —Katharine Cobey

Teresa Barkley's *Labels Quilt* not only reminds us that quilts are the most enduringly popular of American traditional folk arts made by women but also calls up "women's work" of

(clockwise from left)
**Gloria Crouse**
*Tying the Knot*
*Wedding Ensemble*
1996
Plastic rings from
six-pack, rip-stop
nylon selvages
Cape: 36 x 100"
Pants: 40 x 24"

**Gloria Crouse**
*Tying the Knot*
*Wedding Ensemble*
(detail)

**Flora Walters**
*Selective Service*
1995
Wedding rings and
replicas, Merlin's
gold, brass, nickel,
silver, 18k and 24k
yellow gold
36 x 22 x 15"

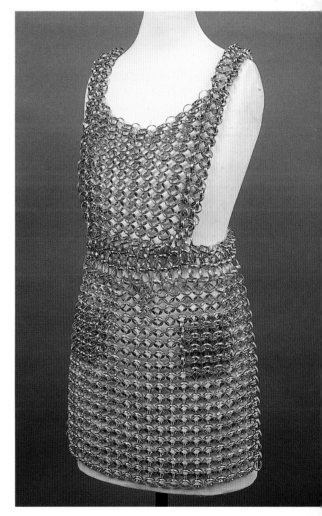

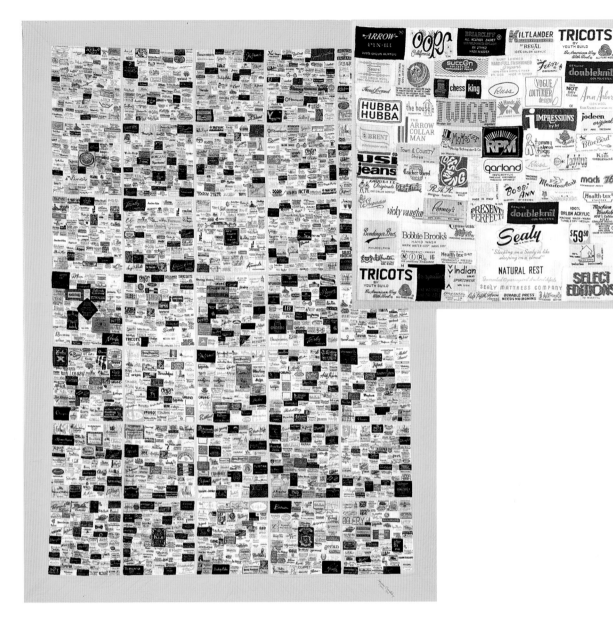

(opposite)
**Willy Scholten**
*Marilyn*
1995
Crocheted
anodized copper
wire, metal hanger
36 x 16 x 2½"

**Teresa Barkley**
*Labels Quilt* (with
detail)
1974
Pieced clothing
labels
95½ x 69½"

another kind: it's usually women who work in sweatshops, making designer dresses for the wealthy and sewing prestige labels into those garments.

The most traditional-looking of the "quilts" in this exhibition is Rik Nelson's *Clear Cut.* Again we have a pun referring to environmental issues: the expedient cutting of old-growth forests in the title juxtaposed against the quilt's real content-recycled household-product containers. Each quilt block is six inches square, and most "recycle" traditional patterns, such as a log cabin, a rail fence, a variety of pine tree variations. A "table of contents" accompanying the piece lists every detergent, fruit drink, motor oil, and sham-poo bottle (among many other kinds) used in the quilt's construction.

**Rik Nelson**
*Clear Cut*
1994-95
Plastic containers
78 x 78"

According to the artist,

> "*Clear Cut* is a sampler 'quilt' and the majority of its patches are traditional patterns. Traditionally, quilts have been made of scraps from a fabric whose larger use was wholly different—a dress, shirt, tablecloth, curtains. My quilt is made from plastic vessels our society treats as scrap—beautifully hued and shaped cruets and vials and miniature amphorae tossed willy-nilly in the dumpster. *Clear Cut* contains over 6,700 individual pieces of plastic and other materials from about 140 different sources.
>
> Traditionally, many quilts have 'stories'—i.e., they commemorate births, christenings, marriages, travels, anniversaries, deaths. Individual patches may have historical meaning or stories associated—e.g., Algonquin Trail, Barbara Fritchie Star, Burgoyne Surrounded, Cross of Temperance, Kansas Troubles, Rocky Road to California, et al. Therefore, I've looked at each patch as a kind of ideograph and organized the patches in *Clear Cut* to provide a narrative:
>
> (1) At the center of the quilt is a Log Cabin patch, and at its core the fireplace, the quilt's brightest piece. But I have taken the traditional patch and converted it into a pulsating gyre.
>
> (2) Surrounding the cabin is a Pine Tree forest. Pine is the most common tree in my neck of the woods, and its variations in quilting, as in Nature, are numerous.
>
> (3) Defending the forest which surrounds the cabin is a Rail Fence. There you have it—your little piece of God's green earth.
>
> (4) At top center in the Rail Fence is a 'gate,' the X of the Garden Path patch. Our domain is the Garden.
>
> (5) Immediately above the Garden Path patch is a Bird's Nest with its pastel eggs. Many birds live in pines. But the border in which this Bird's Nest resides is a Garden Path mutation, a patch I call Logging Road. At its center is the 'high lead,' the single limbless tree at the top of a hill whence cable is strung and all the timber clear-cut below is yanked to the top for loading. This border is like the clear gel that first congeals on a wound.
>
> (6) The outermost ring is an Everlasting border. At two of its corners are withered Pine Trees. Interspersed are Buzz Saw patches. Where the buzz saw has been, the Everlasting turns brown. The buzz saw advances on the green portions where a lone Tall Pine survives; and in the bottom left corner a Weeping Willow and Tree of Life. The buzz saw has been so rapacious it has reached the edge of the world, cutting into the framework itself.
>
> Meanwhile, back at the center of our own personal worlds, we sit by the hearth, comforted by the narrow band of trees we see out the window, safe inside our fenced-off property. All is well. Clear cut."[31]

**Artists almost always respond to their materials.** Rather than forcing an art medium to assume texture, surface, or form, many artists seek materials from the scrap heap that already have those interesting qualities. It's commonplace for artists recycling materials from other uses to say that those materials are less intimidating to them than the proverbial blank sheet of expensive paper. Experimentation is easier if the material is cheap, or

free. But unlike Nevelson, who neutralized her stockpile of found materials by sanding them clean or painting them a uniform color, most artists included in this exhibition treasure each found material's visual contribution to their creations. Without the patina of old paint or rust, or some other surface pattern or texture, most of these materials would be as boring as a new two-by-four.

Without its worn paint, the wood used by Stephen Whittlesey and David Klein in their respective furniture would not be half as interesting. Whittlesey's forms are often guided by his raw materials too. He describes himself as "an archeologist of the backwoods, flea markets, landfills, and dumpsters."[32]

David Klein says that the content of his work "is the remnants of the late, great City of Baltimore. It's the beauty of age. Why should it be buried forever when I can preserve it? Provenance? I've resurrected everything from confectioneries to confessional boxes. What

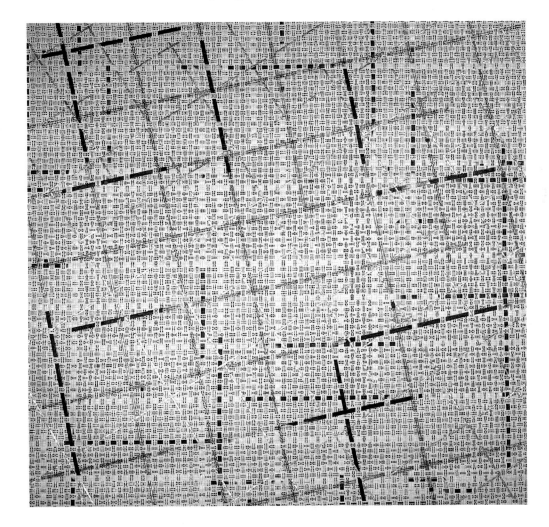

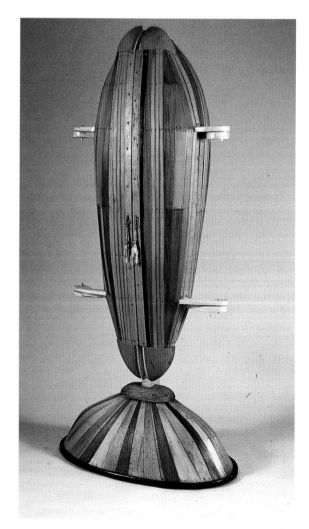

(above and right)
**Stephen Whittlesey**
*Chrysalis Cabinet*
1996
Salvaged wood
72 x 35 x 20"

makes a Klein? Color. Color and texture. I'm driven by color and texture and I go with color as I find it, putting different boards together until they start really looking good."[33]

**Artists use materials that suit their processes.** John Marcoux, educated as a painter but employed as a furniture designer since 1956, constructs furniture from layered newspaper and makes lamps and small tableaus from cut waste tin. Like Marcoux, Kate Hunt finds that newspaper suits her goals in creating sculptural form. Though we think of old newspaper as one of our most plentiful disposable items, in closed landfills papers are known to have survived for decades, still readable. The tight layers of newspaper in both Marcoux's and Hunt's art, like laminated wood, give them strength and durability.

(opposite)
**David Klein**
*Big Bob*
1991
Salvaged wood,
leather, copper
89 x 40 x 19"

(clockwise from
top left)
**John Marcoux**
*Item*
1989
Newspaper, wood
dowels, basswood
top frame
18 x 15 x 15"

**Kate Hunt**
*Something Catholic:
Gold Leaf Bowl*
1994
Newspapers, gold
leaf
7¼ x 18 x 18"

**Chris Berti**
*Red Hill*
1996
Carved brick
6½ x 9 x 3"

"People ask me why I use old newspaper and cardboard in my baskets. I give a variety of explanations. Sometimes I say that I like the convenience of having my materials delivered to my door every morning. Sometimes I say that the valuelessness of the materials encourages me to experiment and to be playful.

Sometimes I say that a faded scrap of newspaper or breakfast cereal carton is worthy of contemplation, and that my baskets are merely presentations of materials with all their baggage of meaning.

Sometimes I say that cartons of breakfast cereal are arresting and beautiful—works of graphic art that I can carry to different levels of imagination for my own purposes. For the materials that I reuse provide starting points for unpredictable processes of transformation.

I want my works to resonate with meanings derived from their unknown or forgotten lives.

I expect that the bottom line is that I use these materials because I like them. They work in the kinds of constructions that interest me."
—Ed Rossbach

Ed Rossbach
*El Salvador Basket*
1987
Cardboard, staples
13 x 13 x 8"

Chris Berti, who usually carves in scrap limestone and wood, discovered a new source of material for sculpture—discarded brick. "The old bricks possess a stone-like quality, rich in color, and contain the texture of composite rock. At the same time, the sculptures are intimate and inviting because of their small scale."[34]

Harold Balazs, equally adept at creating sculpture in formed concrete and developing abstract imagery in glass enamel fused to sheet steel, found an unusual source of material for his enamel art—the enameled lids and side panels of washing machines and dryers. "Having an almost free surface to work on has enabled me to work with more abandon than I may have otherwise dared, and in some cases to be just plain silly. . . . *The Bishop* is a comment on the sometimes absurd nature of 'official documents,' with more than a nod to Saul Steinberg's *The Passport*."[35]

**Harold Balazs**
*The Bishop Has Kept
Score, Affixed His
Seal, and You Are
Found Wanting*
1991
Glass fired onto
drawer panels from
stove, seals are lead
from wine bottles
22 x 19½"

Ron Baron
*Golden Anniversary*
1992
Ceramic plates,
books, baseballs
27 X 13 X 13"

**The new "art supply stores"—consignment shops and thrift stores—flourish today.** Rummage sales, once the mainstay of fundraising in church basements and other forums, have given way to so many garage and yard sales that most city newspapers have a section of the classified ads devoted exclusively to them. Of course, they are of interest to more than artists; people from all walks of life, and seemingly almost all income groups, enjoy the search for something that they didn't know they needed.

Consider the range of places that sell used stuff. Consignment stores usually sell designer clothes or goods that the original owner deemed too valuable to give away to a charity thrift store. Stores selling used books are nothing new, but now there are also stores devoted to used CDs. And thrift stores are flourishing. In recent years small hole-in-the-wall thrift stores, with their jumbled piles of castoffs, have been transformed into well-lighted, orderly shops with clothes grouped on racks by type, size, and maybe color. Many feature changing rooms in which customers can try on their clothing purchases. And the larger stores are no longer found only in recycled grocery buildings: increasingly, Goodwill and Value Village stores, for example, can be found in bustling business districts in new structures built especially for them. These establishments are an important expansion of the reuse of still-usable things as well as an important source of materials for art of the sort seen in this exhibition.

Thrift stores, and artists using castoffs, can reconsume only a small percentage of our throwaways, however. The United States represents only five percent of the world's population, but it produces fifty percent of its solid waste. Through aggressive recycling, we could reduce that appalling percentage.[36]

**Let's look at the truth about recycling.** A recent article in the *Seattle Post-Intelligencer*, reprinted from the *New York Times Magazine,* asserted that "recycling may be the most wasteful activity in modern America—a waste of time and money, a waste of human and natural resources."[37] The spurious arguments cited were quickly countered by both

**Karyl Sisson**
*Blondie #4*
1992
Miniature wood
clothespins, wire
$4\frac{1}{2}$ x $15\frac{1}{2}$ x $15\frac{1}{2}$"

**Ken D. Little**
*Fury*
1983
Leather jackets,
shoes, baseball
gloves, painted blue
jeans, tin, cords,
recycled paper
56 x 90 x 31"

"*North and South Meet and Move West* is about the intersection of two people at a particular place on the map and about the beginning of their journey together. It is about what (baggage?) you bring with you (no matter where you go) and about what happens when the contents of your suitcase merge with the contents of someone else's. It is about making a new map, looking for a collective destination. The handkerchiefs (see the interior of the vessel) are part of my family history. My mother's aunts used what seemed like millions of them. They always seemed to be clean and pressed, ready for action. The postcard is a souvenir. A place my husband has always gone. Every summer. We fell in love there. Now we take our children there. Every summer. As far as the material I used, it's not so much about having chosen materials with a past life but more about the concept of the work driving what needed to be used. I didn't choose the materials; they chose me. For me it is about using the most appropriate material. It is about the physical ingredients helping to define the conceptional contents of the work." —Bird Ross

**Bird Ross**
*North and South Meet and Move West*
1990
Handkerchiefs, maps, postcard, book pages, thread
7½ x 10 x 10"

national and regional organizations that know firsthand that recycling is not only valuable but also good business.

*Curbside recycling programs are a success.* Well-designed and publicized curbside collection programs in typical American suburban communities routinely achieve participation rates of eighty percent or higher. Since 1985, consumption of recovered metals, glass, plastic, and paper by U.S. manufacturers has grown steadily, even as commodity prices for virgin and recycled materials have naturally fluctuated.[38]

*Everyone benefits from recycling.* The greatest environmental benefits of recycling occur in reducing the natural resource damage and pollution that arise in the extraction of virgin raw materials and the manufacture of new products. Materials collected for recycling have already been refined and processed once, so manufacturing the second time around is usually much cleaner and less energy-intensive than the first. Moreover, recycling-based manufacturing reduces the need for strip-mining and clear-cutting.[39]

*Recycling costs less than garbage collection.* When market prices for recycled materials are high, as in 1995, they can offset or exceed the costs of recycling collection. The vast majority of community-based curbside recycling programs are less than ten years old.

**Missy Stevens**
*The Tribe*
1992
Sewing thread,
embroidered in
loop pile
7³/₄ x 7³/₄"

**Michael Stevens**
*Dingo*
1994
Linoleum floor
tiles, pine
95 x 26"

"The materials I use are basic—cloth and thread. The cloth is the foundation which will be covered entirely with a loop-pile embroidery. The thread I use is sewing thread. I discovered as I started making these pieces that the older cotton thread from my mother's and grandmother's sewing box had a beautiful silky sheen that new thread doesn't seem to have. Among these old cotton threads were spools of silk that I had kept because of their remarkable colors but never had been able to use because they had lost their tensile strength. I've discovered that I can use these glorious old silks with my punch-needle because nothing ever tugs on them. Because color is so very important to my work, having the option of using the palette of my stitching ancestors as well as all the thread colors of today allows me more freedom and possibility as I make a thread painting." —Missy Stevens

Over time, as fewer garbage trucks need to be replaced due to increased recycling, garbage collection costs, and hence total system costs, will decrease.[40]

*The market for recycled materials is growing.* New mills making paper for corrugated boxes, newsprint, commercial tissue products, and folding cartons have lower capital and operating costs than new mills using virgin wood. This is why U.S. pulp-paper manufacturers have voluntarily built or expanded more than forty-five recycled-paper mills in the 1990s, and are projected to spend more than ten billion dollars on such facilities by the end of the decade. Recycling, long the lower-cost manufacturing option for aluminum smelters, is also essential to the scrap-fired steel "mini mills" that are part of the rebirth of a globally competitive U.S. steel industry.[41]

*Remanufacturing materials into new products creates jobs.* In Washington state, total recycling employment has increased by about twenty-nine percent since 1992. Part of that job growth has occurred in firms that make recycled-content products, during a time in which thousands of other manufacturing jobs were lost in the state.[42] According to Marilyn Skerbeck, co-president of the Washington State Recycling Association, a May 1996 study by the King County Department of Natural Resources reports that 16,700 people were employed by recycling firms in the state at the end of 1995, and more than 13,000 additional jobs—more than in the entire biotechnology industry of the state—were in companies that manufacture recycled-content products.[43]

**Lisa Ziff**
*Vases*
1996
Sandcast and
polished aluminum
12 x 6 x 4" each

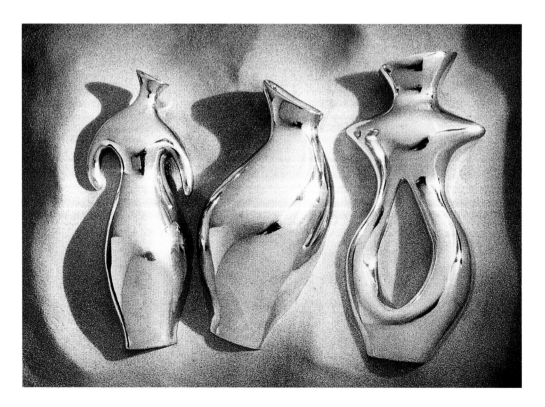

**Deja, Inc.**
*Disruptive Element Agitator Boots*
1996
Soda bottles, metal, magazines, corrugated cardboard, coffee filters, file folders, tire rubber
6 x 3 x 10" each

*We all use more recycled products than we realize.* "In a typical morning, George puts in a load of laundry using Tide detergent (from a thirty percent post-consumer HDPE plastic container), sits down to breakfast pouring Tropicana orange juice (from a thirty percent post-consumer glass container) and eats his Cheerios in handfuls (from a thirty-five percent minimum post-consumer paperboard box) as he reads the (twenty percent recycled newsprint) *New York Times*."[44]

*Design entrepreneurs lead the way in manufacturing new products from old.* The materials from which new products are manufactured are surprising. Who would have dreamed that fleece fiber could be made from plastic pop bottles? Or that attractive sculptural lights (like the Lumalights in this exhibition, designed by Roland Simmons for Interfold) could be made from one hundred percent recycled paper?

Lisa Ziff's sensuously undulating vases, cast from recycled aluminum, are increasingly found in quality gift shops and design stores. Portland, Oregon, designer Colin Reedy and his firm, Metamorph, are among the foremost design innovators in the country. Their highly original designs for chairs and tables made from such diverse materials as plastic "lumber" and sheet stock from recycled bottles, and composite materials incorporating coffee grounds, are prototypes for industrial production.

Another Portland firm, Deja, Inc., founded in 1991 by entrepreneur Julie Lewis, manufactures shoes from such diverse "trash" materials as recycled metal, pop bottles, magazines and cardboard, coffee filters, file folders, and rubber tires.

**Let's not gloat over the success of recycling; there's a lot more to be done.** Despite the proliferation of new products manufactured from refuse, along with the growth in domestic use of these products and the exportation of materials such as recycled papers for reuse, we still recycle less than half of our garbage.

The Environmental Defense Fund tells us that the following amounts of commonly recycled materials are left in our trash rather than sent for recycling:[45]

| Material | Percentage Left | Amount Thrown Away Annually (in millions of tons) |
|---|---|---|
| Newsprint | 54% | 6.0 |
| Magazines | 70% | 1.5 |
| Office paper | 57% | 3.9 |
| Corrugated boxes | 45% | 12.7 |
| Glass containers | 74% | 9.0 |
| Steel cans | 47% | 1.4 |
| Aluminum cans | 34% | 0.6 |
| Plastic pop bottles | 59% | 0.4 |
| **Total (above materials)** | **54%** | **35.5** |

Additionally, yard trimmings make up about one-fifth of our waste nationwide and more than a third of the waste in many suburban communities, particularly in the Sunbelt. Less than a quarter of this material is currently recovered for composting.

**Richard Marquis**
*Toothbrush Propeller Bird*
1980
Glass, mixed media
9½ x 10 x 8"

(clockwise from top)
**Lynn Ludemann**
*Moondoggy*
1996
Metal, glass, wood,
patina, quartz,
battery, clock
movement
18 x 6 x 8"

**Paul Marioni/**
**Ann Troutner**
*Cast Panel,*
maquette (detail) for
the architectural
installation
*Yearbook* 1986
Recycled automobile
headlight glass
28 x 7¾ x 1"

**Margo Mensing**
*Hand Towels*
1991
Embroidered towels,
towel bar
16 x 26 x 3"

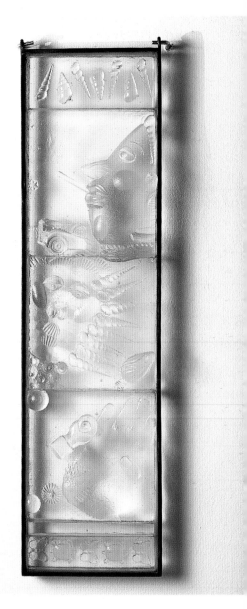

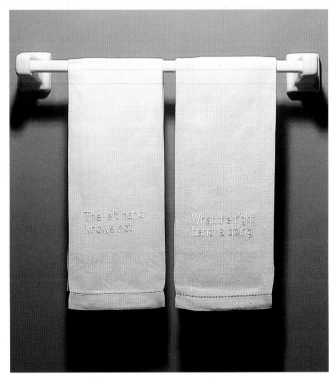

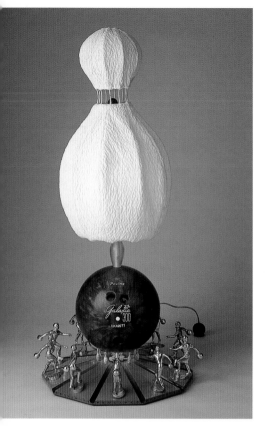

**Rolf Eric Kuhn**
*Pauline's Purported Passionate Patronage Pirouetted Pursuant Personal Proficiency Proximity*
1991-97
Bowling ball, hard maple, plated cast figures, fabric, polychromed steel
32 x 18 x 18"

Suzette Sherman and Peter Stathus, writing in *Refuse: Good Everyday Design from Reused and Recycled Materials*, observe that:

"When we consider the obstacles recycling must overcome, we can marvel that we have achieved even our modest current rate. . . . Also, several states have post-consumer content laws, those of California having had the most impact. By 1995 California had mandated minimum percentages of post-consumer content for glass, paper and certain plastics (twenty-five percent required in HDPE packaging alone). Since California represents ten percent of the total market, this has had a major impact on national demand. Virgin material markets, be warned!

The amount of municipal recycling has steadily increased, with 587 new initiatives in 1993, the last year for which figures are available as of this writing. There are now almost 4,000 collection programs in this country."[46]

**Conclusion.** Even though we have made great strides in recycling in the United States, it is much too early to become smug. According to Victor Papanek, "The United States is far behind most developed industrialized countries so far as re-use, re-manufacturing and recycling are concerned. . . . Sweden and Germany are presently leaders in this race, with Japan rapidly catching up. . . . In Germany . . . automobile companies are financially responsible for taking back automobiles and parts when they are no longer usable. The law further insists that all components of automobiles, TV sets, refrigerators, computers and other large appliances be made from single raw materials (that is: the dashboard can be aluminum, steel, plastic or wood, but it must be made from a single material only) so that the parts can be easily and economically recycled. Similar rules exist in Sweden. The Japanese are about to adopt this policy, since it will lead to more sales."[47]

The consequences of this sort of legislation are far-reaching. Indeed, unless the United States adopts similar legislation, American automobiles will not be allowed on the market in Germany, Sweden, or Japan. Such economic incentives should be widely implemented, because they will stimulate manufacturers to conform.

What else can Americans do as other nations surpass us in solving the global trash glut? Buy less, and use it up. Buy products that are recyclable and that are already made of recycled materials. Reuse, repair, recycle to thrift stores. Make art. Buy art. Get politically active. The future depends on us.

# ENDNOTES

1. Walter Hopps, Ulf Linde, and Arturo Schwarz, *Marcel Duchamp: Ready-mades, Etc., 1913-1964* (Milan: Galleria Scharz, 1964), 24.

2. Ibid., 72.

3. Milton Rugoff, Constance Sullivan, David W. Scott, and Lloyd Goodrich, eds., *The Britannica Encyclopedia of American Art* (Chicago: Encyclopedia Britannica Educational Corporation, 1974), s.v. "Dada," by David W. Scott.

4. Dore Ashton, *A Joseph Cornell Album* (New York: Viking Press, 1974), 6.

5. Ibid., 4.

6. Arnold B. Glimcher, *Louise Nevelson* (New York: Praeger Publishers, 1972), 53.

7. Ibid.

8. Brad Lemley, "Beer, Bricks, and Modern Madness," *Washington Post Magazine*, April 20, 1986, 10.

9. Wrapper for souvenir postcards purchased by the author at the Paper House, Pigeon Cove, Massachusetts, in the 1980s.

10. Seth Shulman, "Houses to Save the Earth," *Parade*, March 3, 1996, 4.

11. "Earthship III," *Real Goods News*, October 1994, 11.

12. James Wallace, "The Gates Mansion: Peeking in the Windows," *Seattle Post-Intelligencer*, September 7, 1997, D-1.

13. Victor Papanek, "The Birth of a New Aesthetic," in *Refuse: Good Everyday Design from Reused and Recycled Materials* (Miami: Arango Foundation, 1996), 56.

14. Suzette Sherman and Peter Stathus, "(Super) Natural Materials," in *Refuse: Good Everyday Design from Reused and Recycled Materials* (Miami: Arango Foundation, 1996), 56.

15. Ibid., 57.

16. Ibid., 58.

17. Ibid.

18. Emily Genauer, cited in Glimcher, *Louise Nevelson*, 56.

19. Glimcher, *Louise Nevelson*, 77-78.

20. Ashton, *Joseph Cornell*, 1.

21. Joy Taylor, in a letter to the author, 1996.

22. Ibid.

23. Ibid.

24. Gaza Bowen, in a letter to the author, 1996.

25. Tina Dunkley, "Helen Cohen's *Miniverse*," text prepared in connection with the artist's solo exhibition at Georgia State University Art Gallery, 1991.

26. David Gilhooly, in a letter to the author, 1996.

27. Daniel Mack, *The Rustic Furniture Companion: Transitions, Techniques, and Inspirations* (Asheville: Lark Books, 1996), 16.

28. J. Fred Woell, in a letter to the author, 1996.

29. Ken Bova, in a letter to the author, 1996.

30. Harriete Estel Berman, in a letter to the author, 1996.

31. Rik Nelson, in a letter to the author, 1996.

32. Stephen Whittlesey, in a letter to the author, 1996.

33. David Klein, in a letter to the author, 1996.

34. Chris Berti, in a letter to the author, 1996.

35. Harold Balazs, in a letter to the author, 1996.

36. Sherman and Stathus, "(Super) Natural Materials," 56.

37. John Tierney, "What a Waste," *Seattle Post-Intelligencer*, July 28, 1996, E-1, E-3.

38. Richard A. Denison and John F. Ruston, *Anti-Recycling Myths* (Washington, D.C.: Environmental Defense Fund, 1996), 1-2.

39. Ibid., 2-3.

40. Ibid., 5.

41. Ibid., 7.

42. Nancy Glaser, "Recycling: The Other Coast, The Other Story," *Seattle Post-Intelligencer*, August 4, 1996, E-1.

43. Marilyn Skerbeck, "Despite Words to the Contrary, Recycling Works," *Seattle Post-Intelligencer*, August 15, 1996, A-15.

44. Sherman and Stathus, "(Super) Natural Materials," 59.

45. Denison and Ruston, *Anti-Recycling Myths*, 11.

46. Sherman and Stathus, "(Super) Natural Materials," 56.

47. Papanek, "The Birth of a New Aesthetic," 61.

# EXHIBITION CHECKLIST

*Height precedes width precedes depth*

**Abrasha**
*Ring*
1996
Steel washers, 24k gold, sterling silver
1$^1$/$_3$ x 1$^2$/$_3$ x $^1$/$_4$"
Courtesy of the Artist, San Francisco, California

**Anni Albers / Alexander Reed**
*Necklace*
1996 (replica after original of ca. 1945)
Sink drain, paper clips, chain
13$^1$/$_2$ x 1 x 3"
Collection of the Joseph and Anni Albers Foundation,
Orange, Connecticut

**Harry Anderson**
*Agitate*
1996
Found objects, glass, brass, copper, steel
51 x 10"
Courtesy of the Artist, Melrose Park, Pennsylvania, and the
Snyderman Gallery, Philadelphia, Pennsylvania

**Clayton Bailey**
*Marilyn Monrobot*
1989
Aluminum, chrome, light
60 x 20 x 20"
Courtesy of the Artist, Port Costa, California

**Harold Balazs**
*The Bishop Has Kept Score, Affixed His Seal,
and You Are Found Wanting*
1991
Glass fired onto drawer panels from stove,
seals are lead from wine bottles
22 x 19$^1$/$_2$"
Courtesy of the Artist, Mead, Washington

**Boris Bally**
*Hurricane Vessel*
1996
Aluminum traffic signs, copper
9 x 25 x 26"
Courtesy of the Artist, Pawtucket, Rhode Island

**Teresa Barkley**
*Labels Quilt*
1974
Pieced clothing labels
95$^1$/$_2$ x 69$^1$/$_2$"
Courtesy of the Artist, Maplewood, New Jersey

**Ron Baron**
*Golden Anniversary*
1992
Ceramic plates, books, baseballs
27 x 13 x 13"
Collection of Bill Arning, New York, New York, through the
courtesy of the Anna Kustera Gallery, New York, New York

**Don Baum**
*The Rider*
1989
Paint by number on canvas, wood
16 x 15$^1$/$_4$ x 7$^1$/$_2$"
Courtesy of the Artist, Chicago, Illinois

**Tony Berlant**
*City Tune*
1988
Metal collage on wood
8$^1$/$_2$ x 7$^1$/$_4$ x 6"
Collection of the Artist, Santa Monica, California

**Harriete Estel Berman**
*Hourglass Figure: The Scale of Torture*
1994
Slim-fast can and cookie tin steel, acrylic
3 x 12$^1$/$_2$ x 13"
Collection of Marilyn Barrett, Bethesda, Maryland

**Chris Berti**
*Red Hill*
1996
Carved brick
6$^1$/$_2$ x 9 x 3"
Courtesy of the Artist, Champaign, Illinois

**Sharon Boardway**
*Don't Forget Me*
1996
Olive jar glass, steel cable
11 x 11"
Courtesy of the Artist, Seattle, Washington

**Ken Bova**
*Daddy's Pride and Joy*
1991
14k and 23k gold, sterling silver, pastel, paper, horn,
pearls, quartz, photo, shell
3$^1$/$_2$ x 2$^3$/$_4$"
Collection of the Artist, Bozeman, Montana

**Gaza Bowen**
*Het Achterhuis*
1995
Suitcase, dollhouse figure/furniture, barbed wire, lighting,
scrim cloth, mirror
14$^1$/$_2$ x 16 x 12"
Courtesy of the Artist, Santa Cruz, California

**Kathy Buszkiewicz**
*Savior*
1996
U.S. currency, wood
1$^3$/$_4$ x 6"
Courtesy of the Artist, Cleveland Heights, Ohio

**Gordon Chandler**
*Buckhead*
1997
Mixed media
36 x 18 x 30"
Collection of the Artist, Carrollton, Georgia

**Randall Cleaver**
*Victorian's Secrets*
1995
Motorcycle fender, oil pump casing, homemade chain
mail, clock
16 x 23 x 5"
Courtesy of the Artist, Landsdowne, Pennsylvania

**Katharine Cobey**
*Loose Ends Dress and Wreath*
1996
Cut and knitted white Glad bags
Dress: 50 x 46 x 6"
Wreath: 12 x 12"
Courtesy of the Artist, Cushing, Maine

**Helen Cohen**
*Sunbeam Toaster*
1996
1950s toaster, ceramic cup and saucer, found objects
8 x 11 x 7"
Collection of the Artist, Groveland, California, through the courtesy of the Braunstein/Quay Gallery, San Francisco, California

**Gloria Crouse**
*Tying the Knot Wedding Ensemble*
1996
Plastic rings from six-pack, rip-stop nylon selvages
Cape: 36 x 100"
Pants: 40 x 24"
Collection of the Artist, Olympia, Washington

**Deja, Inc.**
*Disruptive Element Agitator Boots*
1996
Soda bottles, metal, magazines, corrugated cardboard,
coffee filters, file folders, tire rubber
6 x 3 x 10" each
Collection of Deja, Inc., Lake Oswego, Oregon

**Marita Dingus**
*Basket*
1988
Fabric on plastic
10 x 13 x 13"
Collection of Michele Bucy, Seattle, Washington, through the
courtesy of the Francine Seders Gallery, Seattle, Washington

**Lynn Di Nino**
*Travelin' Man*
1992
Suitcase, gloves
22 x 27 x 20"
Courtesy of the Artist, Seattle, Washington

**Paul Di Pasqua**
*It's What's Inside That Counts*
1996
Found objects
30 x 18 x 15"
Courtesy of the Artist, Chico, California, and the Virginia Breier
Gallery, San Francisco, California

**Robert Ebendorf**
*Brooch*
1994
Windshield glass
2 x 3 x 1¼"
Collection of the Artist, Topeka, Kansas

**Wharton Esherick**
*Hammer-handle Chair*
1938
Hickory, canvas belting
32½ x 20½ x 21"
Collection of the Wharton Esherick Museum, Paoli,
Pennsylvania

**Lisa Fidler**
*Spinning Ouija Brooch*
1996
Mirror shards, thesaurus pages, sterling silver, glass,
dice, taillight plastic
3½ x ⅓"
Collection of Elsie Michie, New Orleans, Louisiana

**John Garrett**
*Wastepaper/Wallpaper*
1994
Colored newspaper ads, Johnson Wax product packaging
120 x 168"
Courtesy of the Artist, Albuquerque, New Mexico

**David Gilhooly**
*Extra Guests at the Last Supper*
1996
Plastics
10 x 20½ x 4½"
Courtesy of the Artist, Dayton, Oregon

**David Gilhooly**
*Floor Show at the Last Supper*
1996
Plastics
8⅞ x 17½ x 3½"
Courtesy of the Artist, Dayton, Oregon

**Laura Griffith**
*Barse*
1993
Cast iron from radiators
20 x 13 x 8"
Courtesy of the Artist, Seattle, Washington, and the
William Traver Gallery, Seattle, Washington

**Polly Harrison**
*Tired Old Dog Basket*
1993
Dog tags, auto inner tubes, cut and twined over welding
rods attached to wood rings
8 x 8 x 17"
Courtesy of the Artist, Cedartown, Georgia

**Tina Fung Holder**
*Martha Necklace*
1995
Safety pins, snap fasteners, glass beads
1/4 x 9 x 8 1/2"
Courtesy of the Artist, Washburn, Wisconsin

**Al Honig**
*Primitive #5*
1995
Mixed media
15 x 13 x 6"
Courtesy of the Artist, San Francisco, California

**Mildred Howard**
*Memory Garden I*
1991
Wood, paint, glass bottles
26 1/2 x 27 1/4 x 31 1/4"
Courtesy of the Artist, Berkeley, California, and the Gallery
Paule Anglim, San Francisco, California

**Kate Hunt**
*Something Catholic: Gold Leaf Bowl*
1994
Newspapers, gold leaf
7 1/4 x 18 x 18"
Courtesy of the Artist, Kalispell, Montana, the Foster/White
Gallery, Kirkland, Washington, and the Joanne Rapp Gallery/
The Hand and The Spirit, Scottsdale, Arizona

**Kimberly Kelzer**
*Go for Baroque Mirror*
1996
Broken mirror, broken green dishes from 1940s and
1950s, beveled glass mirror, grout
44 x 21 x 6"
Collection of Arthur and Diane Dion, Newton Highlands,
Massachusetts

**David Klein**
*Big Bob*
1991
Salvaged wood, leather, copper
89 x 40 x 19"
Collection of the Artist, Baltimore, Maryland

**Sheila Klein**
*Trying once again to make the connection between
all things*
1996
Wire hangers
48 x 64"
Courtesy of the Artist, Bow, Washington

**Rolf Eric Kuhn**
*Pauline's Purported Passionate Patronage Pirouetted
Pursuant Personal Proficiency Proximity*
1991-97
Bowling ball, hard maple, plated cast figures, fabric,
polychromed steel
32 x 18 x 18"
Collection of the Artist, Loveland, Ohio

**Ken D. Little**
*Fury*
1983
Leather jackets, shoes, baseball gloves, painted blue
jeans, tin, cords, recycled paper
56 x 90 x 31"
Collection of The Contemporary Museum, Honolulu, Hawaii.
Gift of the Artist, 1997.

**Lynn Ludemann**
*Moondoggy*
1996
Metal, glass, wood, patina, quartz, battery, clock
movement
18 x 6 x 8"
Courtesy of the Artist, El Granada, California

**Daniel Mack**
*Rugbeater-back Armchair*
1995
Maple saplings, wicker rugbeaters
48 x 26 x 24"
Courtesy of the Artist, Warwick, New York

**John Marcoux**
*Item*
1989
Newspaper, wood dowels, basswood top frame
18 x 15 x 15"
Courtesy of the Artist, Providence, Rhode Island

**Donna Rhae Marder**
*Pinwheel Quilt*
1994
Sewn coffee filters, industrial screen
36 x 48 x 3"
Courtesy of the Artist, Winchester, Massachusetts, and the
Mobilia Gallery, Cambridge, Massachusetts

**Donna Rhae Marder**
*Mother's Tunic*
1995
Sewn 1960s magazines, waxed paper
38 x 30 x 7"
Courtesy of the Artist, Winchester, Massachusetts, and the
Mobilia Gallery, Cambridge, Massachusetts

**Eric Margry**
*Blowup Bracelet with Pump*
1996
Bicycle tire tube, sterling silver
Bracelet: 4 x 3 1/2 x 1"
Pump: 1 1/8 x 8 1/4 x 1 1/2"
Courtesy of the Artist, Mt. Rainier, Maryland

**Paul Marioni / Ann Troutner**
*Cast Panel,* maquette for the architectural installation
*Yearbook*
1986
Recycled automobile headlight glass
28 x 7 3/4 x 1"
Collection of the Artists, Seattle, Washington

**Johanna Nitzke Marquis**
*Hey Now What's That Sound Everybody Look What's Going Down*
1995
Watercolor, mixed media
19 x 12¼ x 2½"
Courtesy of the Artist, Freeland, Washington, and the Elliott-Brown Gallery, Seattle, Washington

**Richard Marquis**
*Toothbrush Propeller Bird*
1980
Glass, mixed media
9½ x 10 x 8"
Courtesy of the Artist, Freeland, Washington, and the Elliott-Brown Gallery, Seattle, Washington

**Margo Mensing**
*Hand Towels*
1991
Embroidered towels, towel bar
16 x 26 x 3"
Courtesy of the Artist, Saratoga Springs, New York

**Rik Nelson**
*Clear Cut*
1994-95
Plastic containers
78 x 78"
Courtesy of the Artist, Cheney, Washington

**Jim Opasik**
*Pan-A-Phant*
1993
Recycled kitchen utensils, pans, pastry bags
36 x 33 x 22"
Courtesy of the Artist, Baltimore, Maryland

**Franc Palaia**
*Eve-Span*
1995
Suitcase, light, c-print, Duratrans
21 x 24 x 8"
Courtesy of the Artist, Jersey City, New Jersey

**Debra Rapoport**
*Rag Lei with Blue Balls*
1988
Shredded newspaper, paint, ribbon, thread, waxed paper, dried botanicals
20 x 24 x 5"
Courtesy of the Artist, New York, New York

**Colin Reedy**
*Loop Seat*
1993
Recycled plastic, stainless steel, rubber nautical bumper
27½ x 22 x 31"
Courtesy of the Artist, Portland, Oregon

**Bird Ross**
*North and South Meet and Move West*
1990
Handkerchiefs, maps, postcard, book pages, thread
7½ x 10 x 10"
Collection of the Artist, Madison, Wisconsin

**Ed Rossbach**
*El Salvador Basket*
1987
Cardboard, staples
13 x 13 x 8"
Collection of the Artist, Berkeley, California

**ROY**
*Mediterranean Bracelet*
1994
Diamonds, bus stop signs
1½ x 6⅝ x ³/₁₆"
Collection of the Artist, Pittsburgh, Pennsylvania, through the courtesy of the Sybaris Gallery, Royal Oak, Michigan, and the Mobilia Gallery, Cambridge, Massachusetts

**Remi Rubel**
*Gold Dress*
1994
Bottle caps
29 x 14 x 40"
Courtesy of the Artist, Albany, California

**Rita Rubin**
*Necklace*
1996
Ancient glass shards, yellow, red, and white gold wire
10 x 10"
Courtesy of the Artist, Los Angeles, California

**Mitch Ryerson**
*Milk Crate Table*
1993
Plastic milk crate, cherry, paduak, wenge, milk bottle caps, epoxy resin, glass, brass
29 x 14 x 14"
Courtesy of the Artist, Cambridge, Massachusetts

**Arturo Alonzo Sandoval**
*Cityscape #3*
1977
16mm microfilm, laundry tag paper, Lurex, cotton edging, eyelets, Velcro
84 x 84"
Courtesy of the Artist, Lexington, Kentucky

**Willy Scholten**
*Marilyn*
1995
Crocheted anodized copper wire, metal hanger
36 x 16 x 2½"
Courtesy of the Artist, San Jose, California

**Roland Simmons**
*Lumalight Lamps*
1997
Acid-free wastepaper
Dimensions vary
Courtesy of the Artist, Cowley, Wyoming

**Karyl Sisson**
*Blondie #4*
1992
Miniature wood clothespins, wire
4½ x 15½ x 15½"
Collection of the Artist, Los Angeles, California

**Kiff Slemmons**
*Protection #2*
1992
Pencils, silver, copper, brass, mirror, leather, horsehair
22 x 9"
Collection of Dale and Doug Anderson, Palm Beach, Florida

**Jeff Smith**
*Hammer in Glass "Emergency" Box*
1996
Wood, glass, metal
24 x 8 x 12"
Collection of Susan and Paul Master-Karnik, Acton, Massachusetts

**Michael Stevens**
*Dingo*
1994
Linoleum floor tiles, pine
95 x 26"
Collection of the Artist, Sacramento, California, courtesy of the Braunstein/Quay Gallery, San Francisco, California

**Missy Stevens**
*The Tribe*
1992
Sewing thread, embroidered in loop pile
7³/₄ x 7³/₄"
Courtesy of the Artist, Washington, Connecticut

**Leonard Streckfus**
*Rhino*
1986
Can, fire hose, golf balls, kettle, mailbox, tire, tricycle parts, wicker horn
30 x 21 x 30"
Collection of Salvatore Scarpitta, Upperco, Maryland

**Brian Swanson**
*Grate-backed Chair*
1994
Roof drain, metal float, auger, motorcycle kickstarter, truck shift-levers
28 x 18 x 19"
Courtesy of the Artist, Kirkland, Washington

**Joy Taylor**
*The Girl I Sawed With You Last Night*
1992
Handsaw, glove
26 x 5 x 2"
Courtesy of the Artist, Red Hook, New York

**Unknown**
*Alcohol Lamps*
Date Unknown
Beer and soft drink cans
5 x 3⁷/₈" each
Private Collection, Seattle, Washington

**Unknown**
*Christmas Tree Garland*
Date Unknown
Chewing gum wrappers
210" length
Private Collection, Seattle, Washington

**Unknown**
*Crazy Quilt*
1900
Tie and dress silks, potato sacks
68 x 66"
Collection of the Whatcom Museum of History and Art, Bellingham, Washington

**Sam Verts**
*Can Console*
1980
Cans, labels, metal armature
34¹/₂ x 49 x 25"
Courtesy of the Artist, Arlington, Virginia

**Flora Walters**
*Selective Service*
1995
Wedding rings and replicas, Merlin's gold, brass, nickel, silver, 18k and 24k yellow gold
36 x 22 x 15"
Courtesy of the Artist, Indianapolis, Indiana

**Stephen Whittlesey**
*Chrysalis Cabinet*
1996
Salvaged wood
72 x 35 x 20"
Courtesy of the Artist, Barnstable, Massachusetts, and the Snyderman Gallery, Philadelphia, Pennsylvania

**David and Roberta Williamson**
*I'm the Guy Who Put the Dots on the Dice*
1991
Recycled sterling silver, antique pin back button, picture from wedding pin, bone dice
3 x 1¹/₄ x ¹/₄"
Collection of the Artists, Berea, Ohio

**J. Fred Woell**
*Pat and Fred Pin*
1992
Plastic, glass, wood, brass, paper
1⁷/₈ x 3 x ¹/₂"
Collection of the Artist, Deer Isle, Maine

**Isaiah Zagar**
*A Day in America*
1996
Plywood, sheet rock, mosaic
96³/₄ x 96³/₄ x 6"
Courtesy of the Artist and the Snyderman Gallery, Philadelphia, Pennsylvania

**Lisa Ziff**
*Vases*
1996
Sandcast and polished aluminum
12 x 6 x 4" each
Courtesy of the Artist, Los Angeles, California

## PHOTO CREDITS

Jay Bachemin (p. 56) • Stuart Bakal (p. 37) • Jeff Bayne (p. 32 top right) • Chris Berti (p. 45 bottom) • Ken Bova (p. 31 top) • Kathy Buszkiewicz (p. 32 top left) • Gary Canaparo (title page) • David Caras (p. 40) • D. B. Cobey (p. 34) • Philip Cohen (p. 33) • Gloria Crouse (p. 35 top & left) • M. Rodrigo del Pozo (pp. 11, 14) • Elvehjem Museum of Art (p. 13) • Isidoro Genovese (p. 19) • Jim Goodnough (p. 42) • Bobby Hansson (pp. 29, 32 bottom right) • Michael Kirkpatrick (p. 26) • Jerry Kobylecky (p. 55 bottom left) • Gordon Kull (p. 27) • Anthony Marino (p. 36) • Richard Marquis (pp. 25 top, 54) • Jock McDonald (p.22) • Dan Meyers (p. 22 top) • Museum of Modern Art (p. 12) • Richard Nicol (pp. 35 bottom right, 51 bottom) • Pipo Nguyen-Duy (front cover, inside front/back cover, pp. 10, 15, 17, 23, 24, 28, 31 bottom, 38, 43, 45 center right, 46–50, 53, 55 top and right) • Dean Powell (p. 32, p. 45 top left) • Colin Reedy (p. 21) • Mary Rezny (p. 41) • William B. Seitz (p. 51 top) • Bruce Shippee (p. 20) • Rod Slemmons (back cover) • Sarah Soffer (p. 31 center right) • Rod Solomon (p. 44) • Sue Tallon (p. 52) • Tom Van Eynde (p. 16 top) • Andrew Wainwright (p. 25 bottom) • Lewis Watts (p. 16 bottom) • J. Fred Woell (p. 30)

## ABOUT THE AUTHOR

Lloyd E. Herman is one of the foremost authorities on the contemporary craft movement in the United States. From 1971 until 1986 he served as founding director of the national craft museum of the United States, the Smithsonian Institution's Renwick Gallery in Washington, D.C. He continues to write about American crafts, and curates exhibitions for circulation by museums and traveling exhibition services. He lives and works in Seattle, Washington.